W9-AJT-541

B is for Bluegrass

A Kentucky Alphabet

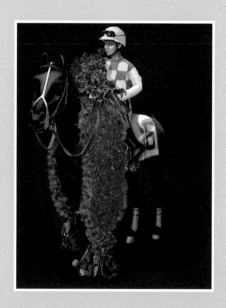

Written by Mary Ann McCabe Riehle and Illustrated by Wes Burgiss

Sleeping Bear Press™

2395 S. Huron Parkway, Suite 200
Ann Arbor MI 48104
www.sleepingbearpress.com

Printed and bound in the United States.

15 14 13 12 11 10

Library of Congress Cataloging-in-Publication Data

Riehle, Mary Ann McCabe, 1959-
B is for bluegrass : a Kentucky alphabet / by Mary Ann McCabe Riehle;
illustrated by Wes Burgiss.
p. cm.
Summary: Presents twenty-six short verses about items characteristic
of Kentucky—one for each letter of the alphabet—followed by a further
description of that person, place, or thing and its importance to the state.
ISBN 978-1-58536-056-7
1. Kentucky—Juvenile literature. 2. English
language—Alphabet—Juvenile literature. [1. Kentucky. 2. Alphabet.]
I. Burgiss, Wes, ill. II. Title.
F451.3 .R54 2002
[E]—dc21   2002004116

B is for Bridget and believing in yourself and believing in this book
E is for Ellen and energy, enthusiasm, and enjoying the moment
P is for Paul and patience and putting up with me and this project

To my family and friends who have taught me
some of life's most valuable lessons.

You have inspired me from A-Z!

M.R.

This book is dedicated to my grandmother, Laura Bullitt
whose lifework came from the love and understanding
of education and its influence on the human spirit.

W.B.

An artist named Audubon
starts us off with A.
He painted many beautiful birds —
ones that won't fly away!

John James Audubon lived near Henderson, Kentucky in the early 1800s. As an artist and ornithologist, someone who studies birds, John James Audubon was able to paint and gather information on many types of birds. The western area of Kentucky, now also known as the Audubon region, is rich in wildlife and natural beauty, making it an ideal setting for the artist.

Do you know the name of the bird painted in this picture? It's the cardinal, our state bird. The male cardinal is red and the female is light brown with just a bit of red on its wings and tail. This difference in color makes them easy to identify.

Aa

Kentucky's nickname, the Bluegrass State, comes from a type of grass that grows well in the soil found mainly in the north-central part of the state.

During the spring large fields of the budding grass may appear blue because the blossoms are bluish-purple. The grass itself is green and the pointy part of the blade looks like the bow of a boat.

Bluegrass is sturdy and well liked by grazing animals which makes it good for pastures.

Not only is bluegrass found in fields and pastures, it is preferred for many lawns and golf courses.

B b

B is for Bluegrass,
across broad fields it's seen
and though it looks the color blue
up close the grass is green.

A Kentucky Colonel is the highest honor given to a person by the governor of the Commonwealth of Kentucky. The Colonels are goodwill ambassadors for the state and have been recognized with this title for their outstanding community service.

World leaders such as President Lyndon Johnson and Prime Minister Winston Churchill, as well as citizens throughout the state and beyond have been given this distinguished title.

Astronaut John Glenn was made a Kentucky Colonel during his mission as the first American to orbit the earth.

Can you think of any other Kentucky Colonels? (Hint: See Letter K!)

Colonel begins with letter C,
though it sounds more like a K.
If you're honored with this title,
it will make your day!

Daniel Boone was a brave frontiersman who loved to explore. He and thirty other skilled woodsmen were members of the Transylvania Company. They set out to discover new territory. Daniel Boone used his knowledge of the outdoors to travel through rough and dangerous terrain.

In 1775, Daniel Boone led pioneers through the Cumberland Gap, a 600-foot passageway through the Cumberland Mountains. They continued their journey into what is now central Kentucky. It was there that Daniel Boone built a fort and established a settlement known as Boonesborough.

Daniel Boone leads us to D
as he led settlers to Kentucky.
Daring to travel through mountains and gap,
finding his way without a map.

E e

Equestrian comes from the Latin root words equus, which means horse, and eques, which means horseman.

Equestrians and horses are an important part of Kentucky's heritage. Horse farms with their walls of stone or wooden rails became a familiar part of the Kentucky landscape soon after the earliest settlers arrived. Lexington and the surrounding region have earned a special place in the hearts of equestrians as the "Horse Capital of the World."

Many equestrians show their horses and compete in a variety of events such as jumping or dressage, an event that requires the rider to direct the horse in precise movements. Another type of competition is cross-country riding. This equestrian event involves riding the horse for several miles through a rugged course that may have natural obstacles such as streams, hedges, and trees.

E is for Equestrian,
a fancy word indeed,
for someone who loves horses
to ride and groom and feed.

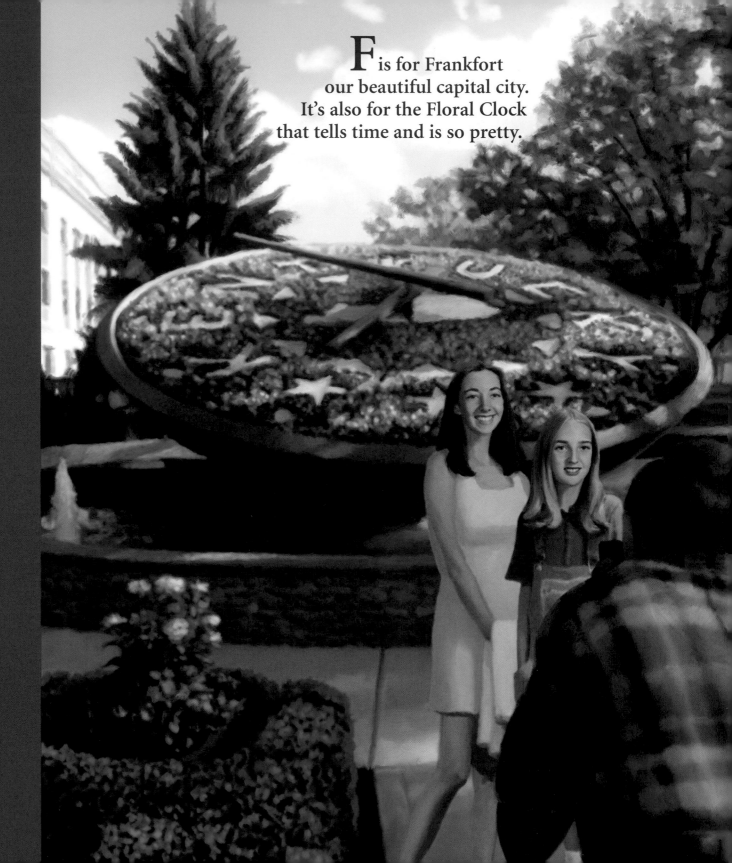

Located along the banks of the Kentucky River, the surrounding scenery and classic architecture of the capitol building make Frankfort one of the most impressive capital cities in the country. The capitol building's focal point is the rotunda with its 212-foot-high dome. This beautiful building was completed in 1910.

Statues of famous Kentuckians such as Henry Clay known as "The Great Compromiser" and Alben Barkley, vice president under President Truman, can be found in the capitol building. Murals depicting Kentucky history are also displayed.

On the west lawn of the capitol grounds is the Floral Clock. Its face is 34 feet in diameter and is made up of over 20,000 plants.

Can you see the difference between the words capital and capitol? Capital refers to the city and capitol to the building. Think "a" for map and "o" for dome.

Ff

F is for Frankfort
our beautiful capital city.
It's also for the Floral Clock
that tells time and is so pretty.

Beginning with the letter G
and glistening like gold —
Goldenrod, the state flower
with color bright and bold.

Goldenrod is a wildflower. Its name comes from the long, slender stem and the golden yellow color of the flower. Goldenrod is often found growing along the roadside. It blooms in late summer and early fall. Goldenrod officially became the state flower of Kentucky in 1926.

Thomas Edison found a way to get natural rubber from the goldenrod plant but the process was too costly to make the product profitable.

Today, people not only enjoy goldenrod for its beauty, but have found many other uses for the state flower. Goldenrod can be used as a tea, a dye, and it can be dried and used in wreaths and other decorations.

H h

Horses of many different breeds can be seen at the Kentucky Horse Park. It is also where you'll find the International Museum of the Horse and a memorial to a famous race horse named Man o' War. This horse won every race he entered except one. In that race Man o' War lost to a horse named Upset.

Kentucky has one of the largest concentrations of thoroughbred horse farms in the world. The thoroughbred is the state horse of Kentucky.

H is for Horses
and a horse park in Kentucky.
If you get to visit there
you'll feel mighty lucky.

Isaac Shelby was the first governor of Kentucky, taking office in 1792 and serving for four years. He was also our fifth governor, taking office again in 1812. He was a well-respected politician and a colonel in the Continental Army.

In 1813 Governor Shelby created a different kind of colonel designation by establishing the honor of Kentucky Colonel.

Isaac Shelby has counties named after him in several different states including Ohio and of course, Kentucky.

I i

Isaac Shelby, the first governor
began his name with I.
He also served as fifth governor.
He must've been quite a guy.

The jockey rides and guides the horse in a race. The special jacket and cap worn by jockeys are called silks. The color and pattern of the silks represent the owner of the horse.

Jockeys can be successful at an early age. In 1875 Isaac Murphy won his first race at age 14. He won the Kentucky Derby three times and was the first ever to have back-to-back wins of that race. He rode for 15 seasons and was known for rarely using a whip or spur on his horse.

Steve Cauthen of Walton rode 488 winners in the 1977 season and was named *Sports Illustrated*'s "Sportsman of the Year." He was only 17 years old. The following year, Cauthen became the youngest jockey to win the Triple Crown.

Jockeys ride on horses' backs
at Churchill Downs and other tracks.
To those who train to race some day J
we dedicate the letter J.

J j

k k K K

K is just one letter
but it may make you think of three.
Think original recipe® or extra crispy™
and you'll think KFC.

Colonel Harland Sanders began what is now Kentucky Fried Chicken® in a small gas station in Corbin. His secret blend of 11 herbs and spices and tasty chicken attracted more and more people. The Colonel could no longer serve the large crowds at his own table in the residence at the gas station so he opened a restaurant across the street. Now there are KFC® restaurants in over 80 countries.

In 1935 Harland Sanders' contributions to Kentucky food and dining were recognized and he was made a Kentucky Colonel. Along with this honor, a bust of Colonel Sanders can be found in the state capitol.

The Louisville Slugger is known as the official bat of major league baseball. The Hillerich & Bradsby Company turns out approximately one million Louisville Slugger baseball bats each year. A major league baseball player can use as many as 100 bats in a season.

Louisville Slugger bats used by baseball legends such as Babe Ruth, Ty Cobb, and Hank Aaron are on display at the Louisville Slugger Museum.

The Louisville Slugger baseball bats are usually made of northern white ash wood. Other woods can be used such as maple but the bat would be heavier. The lighter bats make it easier to swing faster and send the ball a greater distance.

Step up to the plate.
Take a crack at letter L.
If you guessed Louisville Slugger,
you did very well.

Ll

Mammoth Cave is one of Kentucky's most famous natural attractions.

More than 350 miles long, Mammoth Cave is the longest cave in the world. Inside the cave there are five known levels with wide-open rooms. There are even waterfalls, lakes, and rivers inside the caves. Many creatures such as bats, beetles, and even blind fish have adapted to the darkness of the caves and its unique environment.

m

M

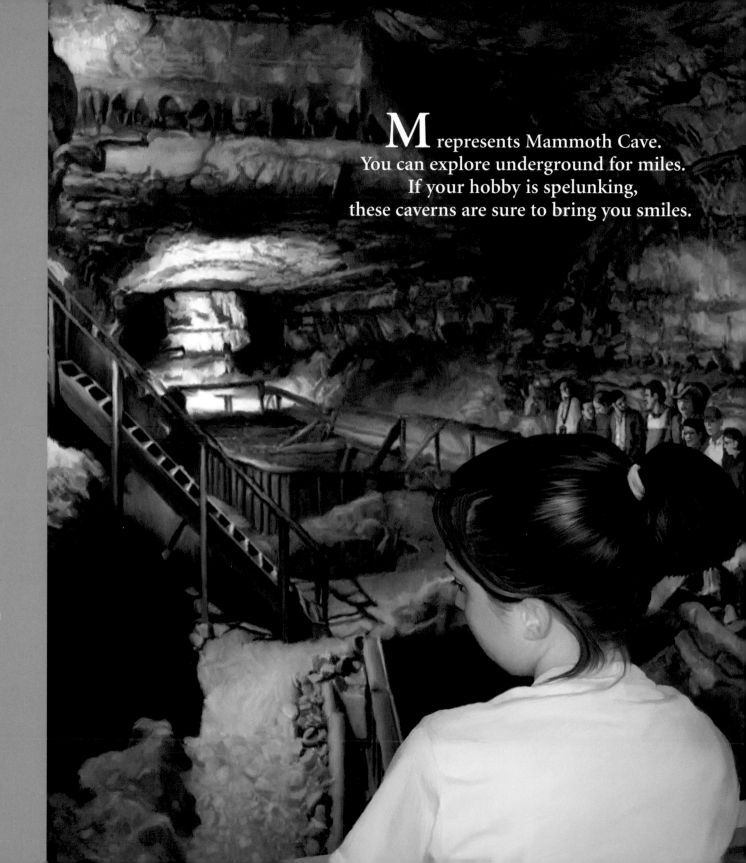

M represents Mammoth Cave.
You can explore underground for miles.
If your hobby is spelunking,
these caverns are sure to bring you smiles.

N helps us notice
some bridges aren't man-made
like the awesome Natural Bridge.
Its beauty will never fade.

N
n

Natural Bridge is made from 900 tons of suspended rock. The bridge is 65 feet high and 78 feet long. Natural Bridge is located in the Daniel Boone National Forest. It has taken nature millions of years to form this awesome sight.

In this eastern area of Kentucky many gorges, steep cliffs, waterfalls, and natural arches have been formed from the erosion of sandstone. These formations are common in this region because the area has strong, thick layers of sandstone mixed with weaker layers. Over many years, erosion has caused the weaker layers to separate, and in some cases, have formed natural wonders such as Natural Bridge.

Three Os in Owensboro,
a city with plenty to do.
Listen to bluegrass music
and try some barbecue.

Originally known as Yellow Banks, Owensboro was later named in honor of Colonel Abraham Owen who fought in the Battle of Tippecanoe.

Because of its location along the Ohio River, Owensboro has always been an important city for trade and transportation. Owensboro is also known for its contributions to culture. Kentucky's third largest city is where you can find the Owensboro Museum of Fine Art and the International Bluegrass Music Museum.

Owensboro hosts the International Bar-B-Q Festival, where local cooking teams compete with their special recipes. Can you imagine 20 tons of barbecue? That's how much is served at the festival each year. Cooks can compete for the Governor's Cup awarded to the "Best Overall Bar-B-Q Cooking Team."

Pp

Pleasant Hill, home of the Shakers, begins with the letter P. Experience the simple life in this community.

Pleasant Hill preserves the customs and lifestyle of a community of people known as the Shakers. They got their name from the trembling done during prayers.

The Shakers arrived in Kentucky in the 1800s and lived a simple, peaceful life. They were skilled craftsmen, making furniture and other useful items. The Shakers are thought to have invented the clothespin and flat broom.

Over 30 original buildings have been restored at Pleasant Hill. Modern-day crafters carry on the skills of the Shakers by demonstrating methods that they would have used years ago.

Paducah, Kentucky, is known as "Quilt City, USA." The National Quilt Museum, also known as the Museum of the American Quilter's Society, is located here. Over two hundred quilts of various styles are on display at the museum.

Quilting has its American beginnings in colonial times. Scraps of fabric were saved and pieced together in different patterns and themes and became warm blankets and treasured heirlooms. Quilts were often given as gifts for special occasions such as weddings or births, and were later passed down to future generations.

Q q

Quilt City, USA
is where you'll find the letter Q.
Quilts, historic sites, and murals
are all here to welcome you.

Roses are draped over the winning horse at the Kentucky Derby, a race that has been called "the greatest two minutes in sports."

Held the first Saturday in May, the race brings people from around the world to Louisville and Churchill Downs. The racetrack was built in 1874 on land owned by brothers John and Henry Churchill. The first Derby was held in May of 1875 to celebrate the opening of the track.

The Kentucky Derby Museum at Churchill Downs showcases the history and the traditions of this exciting sporting event.

R
r

Run for the Roses
that's twice for letter R.
It's the race they call the Derby,
drawing crowds from near and far.

Stephen Collins Foster was inspired to write "My Old Kentucky Home" while visiting his cousin's plantation, Federal Hill, in Bardstown. The song, written in 1852, is Kentucky's official state song. Other famous songs composed by Stephen Foster include "Camptown Races" and "Oh! Susanna."

Sisters Patty and Mildred Hill of Louisville wrote what has become one of the world's most familiar songs, "Happy Birthday to You." Mildred and Patty were both educators and wrote the song in 1893 for their kindergarten students. The song was originally written as "Good Morning to You," with the birthday lyrics added later. "Happy Birthday to You" is one of the most famous tunes of all time.

Take a guess at letter S.
Sing a Song or two.
Songs like "My Old Kentucky Home"
and "Happy Birthday to You."

S s

The tulip tree is the official state tree of Kentucky. In 1994 it replaced the Kentucky coffee tree as the state tree. The tulip tree is a type of magnolia tree. In the spring the tree's yellow blossoms look like tulips, giving the tree its name. The tulip tree can grow to nearly 150 feet tall.

Can you find anything else in this picture that begins with the letter T? How many letter "Ts" are in the poem? (Clue: Even the answer has two in it.)

Standing tall like the letter T
could it be a majestic Tree?
A few more Ts, that would be great
The Tulip Tree is the tree of our state.

The state motto is one of many important state symbols on the Kentucky flag. In the center of the navy blue flag is the state seal. Standing united, a statesman and frontiersman are shown shaking hands with our motto above and below them. Goldenrod, our state flower, is shown below the motto and the words "Commonwealth of Kentucky" are above it.

Kentucky is one of only four states known as commonwealths. The others are Virginia, Massachusetts, and Pennsylvania. Kentucky became our nation's fifteenth state on June 1, 1792.

The state motto begins with U.
"United We Stand, Divided We Fall"
displayed on the flag
to be seen by one and all.

V, very graceful in the sky
chased by girl and boy,
it's our state butterfly,
the vivid Viceroy.

The viceroy is a brilliant reddish-orange color with black outlining its wings. Its markings are not only beautiful, but help keep the butterfly safe from predators. The viceroy has four legs for walking and two small front legs used for eating.

In 1990 the viceroy was designated the state butterfly of Kentucky.

Kentucky has some other special state animals. The state wild animal is the grey squirrel and the state fish is the Kentucky bass. We even have an official state fossil, the brachiopod, a primitive sea animal that looks like a shell.

A narrow trail used to bring settlers through the Cumberland Gap and into Kentucky became known as the Wilderness Road. Dr. Thomas Walker was the first frontiersman to travel the trail. In 1775 Daniel Boone and other explorers would clear and improve the path, bringing more settlers to Kentucky.

By the early 1800s over 200,000 pioneers had traveled it. Part of the Wilderness Road is still preserved in Levi Jackson State Park in London, Kentucky.

W winds us 'round to Wilderness Road,
the first road in the state.
Rough spots made travel slow
though no stoplights made you wait.

Fort Knox is named for Major General Henry Knox who was the first Secretary of War in the United States.

Fort Knox houses more than six billion dollars worth of gold for the U.S. Treasury Department. A bullion of gold looks like a brick. The bullions of gold are stacked in the depository that was built in 1936.

During World War II many important national documents were stored in the vault at Fort Knox for safekeeping. Some of those documents included the Declaration of Independence and the Constitution. These documents have been returned to the National Archives in Washington, D.C., but the gold in Fort Knox remains.

Find the X in Ft. Knox
and you'll find a treasure
where our nation stores its gold
almost too much to measure.

KENTUCKY

Y y

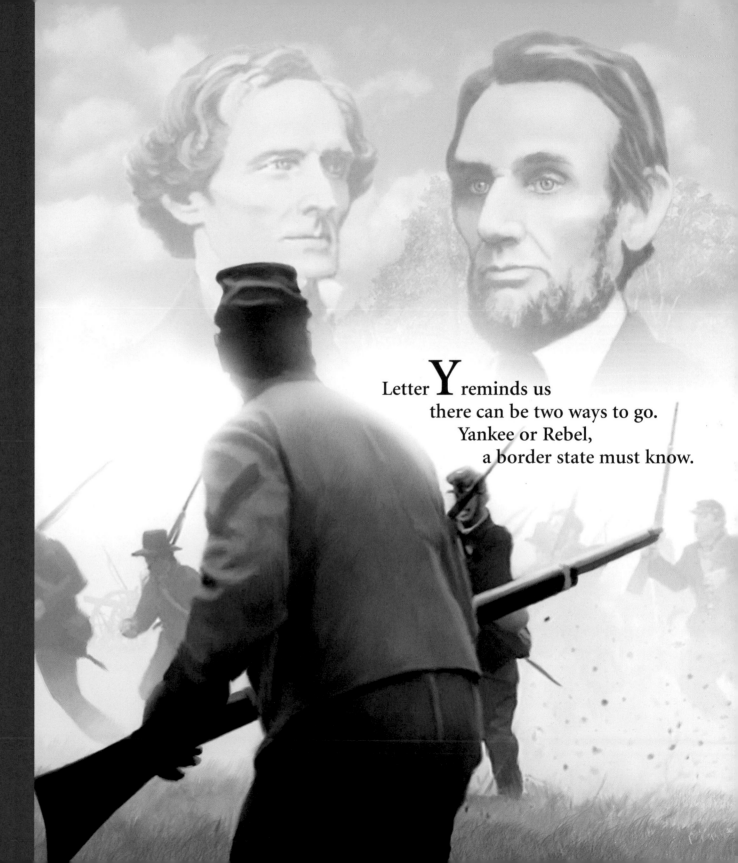

Early in the Civil War, Kentucky tried to remain neutral. Its geographic location gave Kentucky ties to both the North and South. As the war continued, members of the same family could find themselves battling each other, Yankees fighting for the North and Rebels for the South.

Abraham Lincoln and Jefferson Davis, both men born in Kentucky only a few months and a few counties apart, were presidents on opposite sides of the Civil War. Born June 3, 1808, Jefferson Davis led the South as president of the Confederate States of America.

Leading the North was President Abraham Lincoln, born February 12, 1809, near Hodgenville. The Abraham Lincoln Birthplace National Historic Site is a tribute to him. Fifty-six steps lead to the memorial, each step representing a year of his life.

Letter Y reminds us
there can be two ways to go.
Yankee or Rebel,
a border state must know.

How about an underwater zoo where you might see zillions of zoophyte? A zoophyte may look like a plant but is actually a simple invertebrate animal like a sponge or coral. You might find these and thousands of other fresh- and saltwater creatures from around the world at the Newport Aquarium in Newport, Kentucky. Clear acrylic tunnels let you walk through the water while sharks and other sea life surround you.

Looking for animals on land? Many types of animals can be found at the Louisville Zoo including some endangered species such as the Cuban crocodile and the black-footed ferret. As a member of the American Zoo and Aquarium Association, the Louisville Zoo has made conservation of endangered animals an important part of its mission. The Louisville Zoo is the State Zoo of Kentucky.

Z z

Looking for something fun to do?
Why not visit a Zoo near you?
Zigzag along paths and you might see
an animal that begins with letter Z.

A Field Full of Facts

1. What is the state bird? What color is the male? What color is the female?

2. What is an ornithologist?

3. What makes bluegrass look blue?

4. What is unique about John Glenn becoming a Kentucky Colonel?

5. Who was Boonesborough named after?

6. What is the state flower?

7. Who was the first governor of Kentucky? How many terms did he serve?

8. What is the state song? Who composed it?

9. What type of wood is usually used to make a Louisville Slugger baseball bat?

10. What is the state motto? Where can you see it displayed?

11. When is the Kentucky Derby held?

12. What are the cap and jacket worn by a jockey called?

13. Where is the nation's gold stored?

14. What is the state butterfly?

15. How many states are known as Commonwealths?

Answers

1. The cardinal—Red—Light brown with a bit of red on its wings and tail
2. Someone who studies birds
3. The blossoms
4. He was in space when he was made a Kentucky Colonel
5. Daniel Boone
6. Goldenrod
7. Isaac Shelby—Two
8. "My Old Kentucky Home"—Stephen Collins Foster
9. Northern white ash
10. "United we stand, divided we fall."—On the state flag
11. First Saturday in May
12. Silks
13. Fort Knox
14. Viceroy
15. Four

Reference List

The World Book Encyclopedia. 1995.

Peterson, Roger Tory. 1980. *Eastern Birds.* New York: Houghton Mifflin Company.

Kentucky Great Getaway Guide 2000, Kentucky Department of Travel, Frankfort, Ky.

2000 Kentucky Travel Guide, Editorial Services Company, Louisville, Ky.

About KFC [online] www.kfc.com/about/story.htm

Frankfort [online] www.frankfortky.org

Goldenrod [online] www.geobob.com

Goldenrod [online] www.encyclopedia.com

Happy Birthday [online] www.thebirthdaycd.com

International Bar-B-Q Festival [online] www.bbqfest.com

Isaac Murphy [online] www.imh.org/imh/

Isaac Shelby [online] www.politicalgraveyard.com

Kentucky Colonels [online] www.sos.state.ky.us/admin/kycol.htm

Kentucky Derby [online] www.derbymuseum.org

Kentucky Postage Stamps [online] www.postcardsfrom.com/stamp/stamp-ky.html

Kentucky State Parks [online] www.kystateparks.com

Louisville Slugger [online] www.slugger.com

Louisville Zoo [online] www.louisvillezoo.org

Natural Bridge [online] www.r8web.com/boone/geology

Paducah [online] www.paducah-tourism.org

Steve Cauthen [online] www.sportslore.com/watn/cauthen-s.htm [online] sportsillustrated.cnn.com/features/1998/sportsman/1977/

Viceroy [online] www.desertusa.com

Viceroy [online] www.encarta.msn.com/index/conciseindex

Mary Ann McCabe Riehle

Mary Ann McCabe Riehle learned her alphabet and much of what she knows about the state while growing up in Ludlow, Kentucky. She graduated from Xavier University with a degree in Communication Arts and Education. *B is for Bluegrass* is her first children's book. She looks forward to visiting schools across Kentucky to share her love of the Bluegrass State with students.

Mary Ann lives in Dexter, Michigan, with her husband and two daughters. Though she has traveled extensively both in the United States and internationally, she always looks forward to coming home to Kentucky.

Wes Burgiss

Wes Burgiss holds a BFA degree from Transylvania University as well as a BFA degree from the Ringling School of Art and Design. After working as executive creative director for several agencies, he founded his own advertising agency. Today, Wes continues his marketing efforts with Eyemagination, a self-owned company that offers corporations branding and marketing expertise. He also enjoys his role as director of marketing services for Bellarmine University. Happily married and the father of two children, Wes lives in Louisville, Kentucky.